The Capacity To Disappear

Staying Present In Your Child's Life

A Watchful Guide to Child Rearing

The Capacity To Disappear

Staying present in your child's life

A Watchful Guide to Child Rearing

Mary Ellen Dale, Ph.D.

Copyright

Copyright © 2018 by **Mary Ellen Dale Ph.D.**

All rights reserved. This book or any portion thereof may not be reproduced or used in any manner whatsoever without the express written permission of Mary Ellen Dale Ph.D. and Butterfly Typeface Publishing except for the use of brief quotations in a book review.

Printed in the United States of America.
First Printing, 2018

ISBN: 978-1-947656-95-6

The Butterfly Typeface Publishing
PO BOX 56193
Little Rock Arkansas 72215

Dedication

This work is dedicated to every mother who gave it her all,
only to find out it wasn't enough.

"There are two types of people who will tell you that you cannot make a difference in this world: those who are afraid to try and those who are afraid you will succeed."

-- Ray Goforth

Contents

Introduction 15

   Ch 1 - Ways You Can Take Responsibility: 20

   Ch 2 - Ways You Can Communicate Openly: 26

   Ch 3 - Ways You Can Engage With Your Child: 32

   Ch 4 - Ways You Can Spend Time With Your Child 38

   Ch 5 - Ways To Cultivate A Positive Influence Over Your Child 44

   Ch 6 - Signs of Human Trafficking 50

   Hope's Story - A Synopsis: Part I 56

      Life Changes 56

      Associations 56

      Sworn To Protect 56

   Hope's Story - A Synopsis: Part II 62

      Reality 62

      Acceptance 62

      Taken 62

   Hope's Story - A Synopsis: Part III 68

      Honest Talk 68

      Identification 68

      Reinforcement 68

   Hope's Story - A Synopsis: Part IV 74

      A Wide-Awake Nightmare 74

      Suicidal Thoughts 74

      I Just Want It To Be Over 74

   Ch 7 - Ways To Nurture Your Child's Spirit 80

   Ch 8 - Ways to Clear The Air 86

   Ch 9 - Ways To Talk To Runaway Teens 92

   Ch 10 - Ways To Support Your Child 98

   Ch 11 - Ways To Address The Needs Of Children, Self, and Family 104

   Ch 12 - ADHD Implications 110

Ch 13 - Ways To Spot Depression.. 116
Ch 14 - Ways To Regain Power.. 122
Conclusion 129
About the Author 131

Foreword

The Capacity to Disappear is a book written in a conversational style that offers dialogue to caregivers of children, depicting how easy and unintentional it is to mentally disappear from a child's fragile existence. The book (and workbook) presents a window into how a child may negatively internalize situations that parents view as everyday, common, or routine.

The book points out how parents can chip away at a child's individuality which could obstruct normal development. It further opens the door to what has been missing from traditional professional help, honesty. *The Capacity to Disappear* is candid about the problems facing children and the lack of interest given by professionals to the plight of disadvantaged parents, especially those of African descent.

The book guides the discussion from the difficulties of early childhood through the concerning issues of the teenage years. The author addresses parental bias and the need for advocacy for families.

Dr. Dale believes that supporting parents, especially single mothers, could do added good for the family than placing blame on the adverse outcomes of children. In short, the author offers hope for situations that may seem hopeless.

The author's experience of providing therapy in several mental health agencies has given her insight into working with families by supporting and educating them in a safe, non-combative and non-judgmental environment. This approach helped caregivers understand that change is a universal concept and not meant just for the child.

This book discusses runaway causes and behaviors of teens, and the negative effects that running away create; specifically, exploitation, sex trafficking, trauma, and other physical and mental health issues. It also weighs in on how easy it is to disappear even while sharing the same space.

Acknowledgments

To …

My husband Pierre Strachan, for his never-ending love and patience and my son Adisa Alkebulan for his love and enthusiastic support.

L. Bernice Parks who supported me without question in everything I accomplished professionally.

Gionni, Dariyah and Jamese Tarver of The PAST Project who showed interest in my book and provided great comic relief when I needed it.

Introduction

ONCE A PERSON becomes a parent, they have an obligation to understand what their responsibilities are. Many adults feel they have mastered the parenting challenge just by virtue of having a child. This is probably one of the most erroneous ways of thinking as a parent. The life of a child is so precious that you cannot leave it to just being, it has to have a purpose, a goal, a definitive outlook on what parents want the end result to look like.

Children may become confused over the simplest things, a statement, an attitude, a gesture, or an indiscriminate sigh, all done at the wrong time. How children process their feelings has a lot to do with how comfortable they are with how parental instructions are given, or, the lack thereof. One of the easiest things in the world is for a child to feel confused about instructions based on how they are presented. Have you ever talked to your child only to be met with a stare of bewilderment? He or she has no clue as to what you are saying to them or asking of them. Only after a careful breakdown of the instructions given, can a child start to feel like they understand perfectly what they are being told or asked to do. Consider a mother or father who has limited patience, not just with the child, but with everything that appears to take their time away from something that has to be done? A child steps in to ask a question, and they are met with a parent who feels the tension of being taken away from a serious and important project.

Consequently, if not steered in the right direction, the child feels hurt and reprimanded even though technically, you haven't done anything wrong. When your child bows his or her head and walks away, you simply go back to what you were doing while the child internalizes what happened. It is quickly forgotten on the surface, and the child goes back to playing. The feeling of hurt that you imposed on the child, is pushed to the back and the child deals with it no more, at least for the moment. Children are like little machines that are constantly running. You, as the parent, input the data and they work to process it, then their brain disseminates the results of the inputted information. What comes out as a result of the input and dissemination, has a lot to do with the behavior, good or bad. Look at it this way; even if you input good information, environmental variables are pulled into the processing before the data is distributed. This is where all those "sit down," "wait a minute," "tell me later," and "forget it" comments come into play. First to the heart, and then to the expression of behavior.

You may be asking, how this has anything to do with how a child behaves or how a child disseminate information? You will have to consider that a child has no information until it is instilled or put into them. So, a smooth transition of information, with comforting and pleasurable variables is received satisfyingly, therefore, processed with a pleasing attitude. I certainly don't have to tell you that if something is pleasant and satisfying, the results will be different than the results of discomfort and hurt. That outcome then would be more damaging and the behavior a little more strained. Can you see it? If not, ask yourself why, at such a young age, does your child appear irritated with things that might make other children happy?

Misunderstanding also has a great deal to do with why children's responses may appear negative. For instance, not appreciating a particular toy you bought when they specifically told you what they liked more. You know, the one you didn't hear them tell you about because you were either busy or doing something not related to parenting. It is normal for a child to become sad over something they wanted and didn't get, perfectly normal, but it should not be something where the child's behavior becomes destructive. This type of behavior happens when the child feels misguided or has developed a pattern of mistrust due to previous situations that did not manifest itself the way it was promised, or even believed. When a child is scared, and that fear is not taken seriously or is overlooked due to the unavailability of personal interaction, everything becomes confusing, especially to the child who doesn't really know how to handle their feelings.

The child, for all intent and purposes, doesn't quite understand why they feel the way they do either.

It is not unusual for a parent to misunderstand a child's behavior, which of course we know now, are based on the child's feelings about particular incidents, statements, or personal parental behaviors from both mom and dad, (moms especially), who deems the child's behavior as problematic. Once mom feels unheard by her child, who, by the way, maybe fighting her own feelings of insecurity, becomes the irresponsible parent, because they begin to believe that some of their child's behavior stems from things unrelated to parenting, home, love, and discernment. It's no wonder mom feels unheard. She may chalk it up to the child being out of control, or being unable to pay attention at the appropriate time, or she may feel that she is not hard enough on the child to invoke the kind of attention she feels she needs from the child. Rarely, and believe me when I say this, rarely does the parent say to themselves, maybe I am not approaching my child appropriately when I need something from them. Or, maybe I am not giving my child enough attention. Most mothers who spend their time at home each day, feel that all of their time is devoted to the child. This thinking could be the bases for continued parenting done through love, but totally misses the mark of creating an authentic and measurable bond with the child, one that creates a wholesome atmosphere, clear understanding, and expectations for the little one. I am not suggesting that mothers around the world are not good parents, I am simply saying that we don't always understand what we unconsciously do to our children. We love them, we provide for them, we do everything we can to make sure they have a good home and everything they need, but we never think about how a child obtains and convert our communication with them and how they may comprehend instructions.

This guide and workbook serve to reinforce the principles shared in the book. We encourage you to read the book and use this workbook/journal to help you sort through the challenges.

Let's Get Clinical

RESPONSIBILITY

Chapter One

Information You Can Use:

Perception is a huge part of what makes up who we are. Our belief system is predicated on how well we navigate through the rough times in our lives, what we experienced and what we pass on to our offsprings.

Questions To Consider:

- Have you taken responsibility for your child's misunderstanding?
- Did you encourage your child to use words to express feelings?

Tools You Can Apply:

- Listen
- Communicate Appropriately
- Ask Questions
- Understand

Ch 1 - Ways You Can Take Responsibility:

No two children think alike. It doesn't matter if they are raised by the same parents or had access to the same information. Each child may hear the same thing but will attach his or her own experience to what they hear.

Thus, personal views and beliefs of the parent(s) may not mirror what the youth perceives (who may institute their perspective to the information), neither may be what the parent meant. Taking responsibility means asking your child what they heard you say, or how they feel about what just happened?

Be clear about what you say and make sure it is understood. If you don't, you may hear about it later and won't have a clue as to when and how the breakdown in communication occurred.

Journal below experiences you may have already had that deals with perspectives drawn from personal experiences.

Journal Your Thoughts Here:

Journal Your Thoughts Here:

Journal Your Thoughts Here:

Journal Your Thoughts Here:

Let's Get Clinical

MOTHER BLAMING

Chapter Two

Information You Can Use:

Honesty has always been the best policy when dealing with a broken or split family. The fragmented chatter may cause a stream of hard feelings, hurt and bad attitudes from both parent and child. Mothers may have, what they feel, is a legitimate reason for not being honest about things that concern their children. Misinformation may leave a child feeling dismissed, not taken seriously or the feeling of not being important to the family. One of the results of this type of situation is the daughter begins to form an inability to take correction from her mother, especially when the truth is obtained from an outside source.

Questions To Consider:

- What 'wrong' information have I communicated to my child?
- Was keeping a secret the only way I could have handled my uncomfortable situation?

Tools You Can Apply:

- Be Honest
- Be Loving
- Be Present

Ch 2 - Ways You Can Communicate Openly:

Daughters may form an inability to take correction from their mother if they believe their mother has not been honest.

When a child spirals out of control, they can blame their mother for not being the mom that they want her to be.

A child's perspective may be skewed based on misinformation or perceived deceit.

Communication reduces the chance of unnecessary hurt and distrust.

Journal below your experience with misinformation and how sharing could have been handled.

Be honest.

Journal Your Thoughts Here:

Journal Your Thoughts Here:

Journal Your Thoughts Here:

Journal Your Thoughts Here:

Let's Get Clinical

MISSING FATHER

Chapter Three

Information You Can Use:

Fathers play an enormous role in the life of a child. It doesn't matter whether the father is home, absent, shows no love, or is non-existent, the child is very much aware of the effects that arise from each position. At-home fathers who never find the time to be in his child's life is no better than the father who is permanently absent. If fathers don't realize their roles as loving parents as well as providers, the child suffers. The child with a father who shows no love, nurses this tremendous void that eats away at their belief in a whole family system and makes them question their self-worth.

Questions To Consider:

- Are you consistent in your child's life?
- Are you complacent regarding your child's activities, experiences and need to connect?

Tools You Can Apply:

- Be Aware
- Be Consistent
- Be Honest
- Be Real

Ch 3 - Ways You Can Engage With Your Child:

At-home fathers who never find the time to be in their child's life are no better than the father who is permanently absent.

Fathers can make the difference in whether a child seeks the love of a stranger, over the vacant love of a father.

This is especially true for girls. Fathers stay present to assure that their daughter knows how she should be treated by a man.

Having a positive model for such a relationship can ensure a healthy start and standard for appropriate expectations.

Journal Your Thoughts Here:

Journal Your Thoughts Here:

Journal Your Thoughts Here:

Journal Your Thoughts Here:

Let's Get Clinical

INTERNAL TRIBULATIONS

Chapter Four

Information You Can Use:

It takes very little effort to confuse a child and keep them from wanting to stay the course, when you, as a parent, continue to make no sense to them.

Providing no explanations, no breaking down instructions, no love mixed with correction, and no positive affirmations when they do things well on their own, is a recipe for mental and behavioral scarring.

Questions To Consider:

- Do you know the importance of caring for your child's emotional well-being?
- Are you actively involved in your child's life?

Tools You Can Apply:

- Watch Your Child
- Guide Your Child
- Keep Trying With Your Child

Ch 4 - Ways You Can Spend Time With Your Child

To help your child feel connected to you, plan events that are unexpected but age-appropriate fun.

Have an open-door policy with your child. Make it easy for them to knock on your door to talk or to just be close to you.

Make sure your child understands why you cannot be present at a particular event and be honest about the reason.

Leave individual notes and daily affirmations so that your child knows you were thinking of only of them.

Encourage your child to express those things that hurt them or make them feel uncomfortable, then show that you understand. Give words of encouragement and reassurance to help them overcome the problem.

Respectfully confront incidents and stand up for your child.

Make sure your child understands your instructions and don't criticize them if your instructions were not clear to them.

Journal Your Thoughts Here:

Journal Your Thoughts Here:

Journal Your Thoughts Here:

Journal Your Thoughts Here:

THE CAPACITY TO DISAPPEAR

Let's Get Clinical

Mother-Daughter Relationship

Chapter Five

Information You Can Use:

Of all human attachments, the most complex, and most heart wrenching is the mother-daughter relationship. Part of why that is so is because the role of a mother is the most difficult there is. Women who are mothers are judged more by their parenting "successes" or "failures" than by any other areas of their lives and held much more accountable for them than fathers are.

Unless a mother purposefully reflects on notions of what is best for her daughter, she may have trouble distinguishing her desires and feelings from those of her daughter.

Questions To Consider:
- What influence do you have over your child?
- Are you helping your child gain her own autonomy and individuality?

Tools You Can Apply:
- Set Boundaries
- Explain Boundaries
- Adhere To Boundaries
- Don't compete

Ch 5 - Ways To Cultivate A Positive Influence Over Your Child

Your child is not your property, he or she is a gift from God to be loved and protected. When treated as such, relationships are stronger.

Understandably, the role of a mother is the most difficult there is and although daughters mimic their mother's behavior early-on and may wish to be exactly as her mother; the teenage perspective often competes with their mother's views.

The teen may view their mother as uninformed, weak and jealous of their youth.

Don't be fooled by this attitude.

As your child gets older, use your creativity to show them how important they have become in your life.

Journal Your Thoughts Here:

Journal Your Thoughts Here:

Journal Your Thoughts Here:

Journal Your Thoughts Here:

Let's Get Clinical

HUMAN TRAFFICKING

Chapter Six

Information You Can Use:

Human sex trafficking is known today as modern-day slavery. Human sex trafficking is the recruitment, harboring, transportation, provision or obtaining of a person for the purpose of a commercial sex act, in which a commercial sex act is induced by force, fraud, or coercion or in which the person is forced to perform such an act is under the age of 18 years old. Victims include very young children, teenagers, boys, and girls. The Trafficking Victims Protection Act of 2000 (TVPA) defines it as "Severe Forms of Trafficking in Persons."

In today's urban areas, most teenage girls have encountered, or know of, at least one finesse pimp and can identify a trap house in their neighborhood.

Questions To Consider:

- Is your child desperate for someone's love?
- Can you identify with the story of Hope?
- Do you know the signs of a trafficked victim?

Tools You Can Apply:

- Educate Yourself About Sex Trafficking
- Educate Your Child About Sex Trafficking
- Share Your Knowledge With Others
- Know Where Your Child Is

Ch 6 - Signs of Human Trafficking

To learn more about signs of human trafficking, use this link for information. https://polarisproject.org

Sex trafficking is prominent and widespread. Parents must arm themselves with knowledge and pay attention to signs hidden in plain sight.

Finesse pimps are in your church, at the library, outside your child's school, at recreation centers, and anywhere your child may go. Finesse pimps look like the guys of whom your teen daughter may dream. Many are handsome, drive nice cars, and they're super charming and helpful.

They are your child's knight in shining armor. If your child is not receiving what they need at home, such as feeling loved, secure and wanted, they are the perfect choice for these villains to prey on them.

Although you love your child, the key is to make sure they know it and feel it.

Journal Your Thoughts Here:

Journal Your Thoughts Here:

Journal Your Thoughts Here:

Journal Your Thoughts Here:

A Case Study

Hope's Story

Subtitles:

Life Changes
Associations
Sworn To Protect

Questions to Consider:

- What drove Hope to find love elsewhere?
- Was Hope's mom aware of how Hope felt?
- Were there things that Hope's mom should have noticed?

Tools You Can Apply:

- Initiate Shared Feelings
- Initiate Open Dialogue
- Initiate Safety

Hope's Story - A Synopsis: Part I

Hope's story is one of hurt, fear, disappointment, and betrayal. It is plain to see that the initial issues Hope dealt with didn't come from just one source. Mom's part in Hope's decisions is the obvious one, but they are not the only ones

After leaving home, Hope's dad made no effort to contact Hope although he knew how much she loved him and how he influenced her dependence on him. If mom refused to allow his visits, he could have reached out to Hope at her school or consulted legal alternatives.

The man in the store was recruiting for his business and only had expectations of filling a quota.

Compassion has no place in the industry of human trafficking.

This pimp's recruitment policy was to create trust and provide a calm and loving illusion.

Journal Your Thoughts Here:

Journal Your Thoughts Here:

Journal Your Thoughts Here:

Journal Your Thoughts Here:

A Case Study cont'd...

Hope's Story

Subtitles:

Reality
Acceptance
Taken

Questions to Consider:

- What were Hope's other options?
- Why were signs of grief not addressed by Hope's family?

Tools You Can Apply:

- Responsibility concerning grief
- Display of changes
- Lack of self-expression

Hope's Story - A Synopsis: Part II

Hope cried for hours after being told of her father's absence. She refused to eat, stayed in her room, and her grades were affected.

There was no lifeline for Hope; she was sinking fast.

Those in a position to help her didn't pay attention to or ignored her signs of grief.

Hope's sister didn't keep an eye on her 12-year-old sibling while in the store.

Journal Your Thoughts Here:

Journal Your Thoughts Here:

Journal Your Thoughts Here:

Journal Your Thoughts Here:

A Case Study cont'd...

Hope's Story

Subtitles:

Honest Talk
Identification
Reinforcement

Questions to Consider:

- Why was Hope not prepared?
- Were there things Hope should have Known?

Tools You Can Apply:

- Initiate The Conversation
- Remove Fear From Dialogue
- List Potential Risks

Hope's Story - A Synopsis: Part III

Not all pimps deal in adult prostitution. Many drug dealers have transferred their dealing skills to the recruitment and prostitution of minors.

Dealing young boys and girls is safer than dealing drugs, because having a child in your car, is far safer than having drugs if stopped by the police.

Youth are programmed to comply, some out of fear, others out of uncertainty. In the case where the child feels overwhelming love for her self-selected "boyfriend," there is no desire to betray his trust.

It is imperative that love is given freely in the home and shared by everyone. Every child needs to feel love from their parents and other family members.

Journal Your Thoughts Here:

Journal Your Thoughts Here:

Journal Your Thoughts Here:

Journal Your Thoughts Here:

A Case Study cont'd...

Hope's Story

Subtitles:

A Wide-Awake Nightmare
Suicidal Thoughts
I Just Want It To Be Over

Questions to Consider:

- How do you handle hurt?
- How do you reverse negative thinking?
- Where is your safe place?

Tools You Can Apply:

- Initiate meaningful conversation
- Initiate talk about anger
- When to run

Hope's Story - A Synopsis: Part IV

When reality comes to light, fear intensifies. Incongruency heightens, and love and fear become an internal fight. The younger the victim, the harder it is for sensible reasoning.

Cognitively, the child tries to hold onto the things that provide the most comfort. When the situation can't be understood, the safest thing to do is ignore the cause of the fear and step up whatever feels secure.

This internal fight can often paralyze the child and cause further damage to their self-worth. Early social training and community awareness is a necessary part of development.

Hope walked into a nightmare with her eyes wide open. By the time she realized she was in trouble, it was too late.

She was not concerned about how to end her predicament; she just wanted it all to be over.

Journal Your Thoughts Here:

Journal Your Thoughts Here:

Journal Your Thoughts Here:

Journal Your Thoughts Here:

Let's Get Clinical

THE SPIRIT OF A CHILD

Chapter Seven

Information You Can Use:

As parents, the first thing to realize is that Hope's spirit had been broken long before she left home the first time. Hope was a victim of someone else's inadequate parental functioning. She had no say in the type of family or situation she was born into, of course, no one does. Hope only knew, what every child knows, that she had feelings that could be hurt or made happy. She believed her family chose to hurt her.

The love she had for her father was not only interrupted but shattered. Hope had no way of knowing that one day her dad would ever come home again. Hope's mother never took into consideration how her actions would affect Hope; she only knew that Hope and her dad spent a lot of time together, time that she desired for herself, and she argued with him about their relationship. She may have wanted to show her authority to Hope.

Questions To Consider:

- Is your child's spirit broken?
- What can you do to repair it or keep it intact?

Tools You Can Apply:

- Share Your Story
- Share Your Love
- Share Your Time

Ch 7 - Ways To Nurture Your Child's Spirit

Different perspectives on life are drawn from various functions. Viewpoints are made up of specific experiences, good or bad. How a child develops feelings, closeness, and attachments to family members are determined by time spent together, the ability to communicate with one another, and actions that show a loving disposition.

Children expect to be loved, protected and cared for. They are not built to handle discord nor are they able to rationalize and appropriate issues beyond their competencies.

Therefore, parents have an important role in the life of their children that is often taken for granted. It is not hard to dismiss and discourage a child.

Journal Your Thoughts Here:

Journal Your Thoughts Here:

Journal Your Thoughts Here:

Journal Your Thoughts Here:

Let's Get Clinical

MISCONCEPTION OF CARE

Chapter Eight

Ch 8 - Ways to Clear The Air

Information You Can Use:

I believe Hope suffered from posttraumatic stress and an adjustment disorder with anxiety and depression. More time spent with her by the mental health professionals could have produced a more accurate diagnosis that may have better directed their treatment and decisions.

When conditions are not treated, or if the wrong diagnoses are made, it leaves the person suffering in a longer state of anguish. The worthlessness Hope felt, did not allow for a reason, or even open and meaningful dialog.

One of the best ways a parent can regain control with their child is to apologize for the hurt they imposed.

Children feel safest when they know they can count on their parent to not only protect them physically but to protect their mental and emotional self.

The worthlessness Hope felt, did not allow, for reason, or even open and meaningful dialogue.

Questions To Consider:

- What behaviors does your child display?
- What behaviors don't your child display?

Tools You Can Apply:

- Ask Questions
- Ask Deeper Questions Often
- Ask Questions Often and Expect Answers

Journal Your Thoughts Here:

Journal Your Thoughts Here:

Journal Your Thoughts Here:

Journal Your Thoughts Here:

Let's Get Clinical

Trauma & Treatment for Clinicians

Chapter Nine

Information You Can Use:

Professionals and parents who work with sexualized and runaway teens would be served well to sit down and have a massive discussion on the reasons why children, at such a young age, choose running away as an option for relief from despair.

Questions To Consider:

- Have you considered the reasons behind the child trauma?
- Are you confused about the situation?

Tools You Can Apply:

- Ask why
- Ask how
- Ask what

Ch 9 - Ways To Talk To Runaway Teens

Teens run away as a last resort. Few teens leave for trivial reasons. Even the teen that meets a boy and has a desire to spend all her time with him, runs away from more than just a desire. As hard as it is for parents to believe otherwise, teens need parental support, honesty, and trust. As unpleasant as it is to hear that your child has been molested by a family member or friend, the child should always get the benefit of the doubt. When they don't get this at home, it leaves a pain-filled void. For each time they are called a liar or told they let it happen, it increases the degree of trauma until it is layered with multiple reasons for fear, distrust, and the feeling of worthlessness tied to hopelessness. Suicide starts to look more like a solution than hearing hurtful words or even words of encouragement. Often trauma is expressed through bad behavior, and ultimately, therapy can become a tooth-pulling event. Clinicians should spend more time creating trust than trying to find out exactly what happened. Once trust is established, the client will want to tell you what happened. Let the client lead you. Be patient.

Help your youth journal true feelings without reacting to things you don't agree with, understand or think odd.

Journal Your Thoughts Here:

Journal Your Thoughts Here:

Journal Your Thoughts Here:

Journal Your Thoughts Here:

Let's Get Clinical

Understanding Family Dynamics

Chapter Ten

Information You Can Use:

A dysfunctional family who refuses to assist their child in healing could make it difficult to find progress. It is imperative to work with the family to gain assurance that the family is on board in the healing process. If they are not, it could be difficult for the child to overcome barriers that will hinder their growth and lead them into a better direction for their lives.

Families should be an important part of the process, especially the ones who are not invested.

Questions To Consider:

- Can you identify family dysfunction?
- Are you on board with the healing process?

Tools You Can Apply:

- Support Your Child's Efforts
- Support Your Child's Emotional Needs
- Support Your Child's Social Needs

Ch 10 - Ways To Support Your Child

First, be honest. Regardless of how you feel, show the child that they are important. Reassurance is necessary when a child feels discouraged and beaten down.

Each family has its own culture, rituals, and ways of being. Many families cannot identify their dysfunction because it is a normal part of their lives. Should someone enter with a different way of being, the family becomes annoyed. Professionals must be able to recognize or identify parts of the culture. When meeting a family for the first time, it is important to be able to self-modify to understand how to deal with that family. No judgment.

As soon as possible, point out whatever you see good in the family. Compliment good behavior and make them feel comfortable with your presence. Make sure you mention that the teen gets her identified good qualities from her mom. Never point out the family's deficiencies unless you have prepared them to hear what you noticed.

Have an escape plan for explosive situations.

Journal Your Thoughts Here:

Journal Your Thoughts Here:

Journal Your Thoughts Here:

Journal Your Thoughts Here:

Let's Get Clinical

THE NEEDS OF A CHILD

Chapter Eleven

Ch 11 - Ways To Address The Needs Of Children, Self, and Family

Information You Can Use:

All teens, whether gay, lesbian, straight or otherwise, want to be safe, to pursue a happy childhood, grow and develop into productive citizens. It is chaos when these things are not extended to those who have less than others or are different. When Jesus said "love one another" he never used the word *except*.

What teenagers want is simple, and I haven't met a teen who didn't want it. Teens want love and acceptance. Some won't take it because of how it is presented to them, or because they feel it is unattainable. Read the book to see other important details teens need.

Questions To Consider:

- Have you stopped to consider what your child wants/needs?
- Have you stopped to address your personal wants/needs?

Tools You Can Apply:

- Recognize Your Child's Needs
- Recognize Your Needs
- Recognize Your Family's Needs

What teenagers want is simple, and I haven't met a teen who didn't want it. They want what they need, love and acceptance. Some teenagers feel it is unattainable.

They spend much time trying to get it at home, and when they don't feel they have it, they will look elsewhere and are often unprepared to recognize real love from the phony feel-good kind. This leads to a parade of hurtful situations both inside and outside the home.

Teens want to be needed, they want to be a valued part of the family. Assign chores, reward good behavior, ask them how they feel, and include them in important family situations and discussions. Of course, parents have the final decisions about the household, but your teen's input makes the process enjoyable and fair to them.

Teens need socialization. If the child is not allowed to interact with peers, you are creating room for disaster. If you are concerned about bad peers, then guide or provide your teen with the right environment to socialize, i.e., church, youth organizations, sports or other organized activities. This is important for your teen and for your peace of mind.

Journal Your Thoughts Here:

Journal Your Thoughts Here:

Journal Your Thoughts Here:

Journal Your Thoughts Here:

Let's Get Clinical

COMMON SENSE FOR CLINICIANS

Chapter Twelve

Ch 12 - ADHD Implications

Information You Can Use:

Many professionals see ADHD behaviors as only a few behaviors, thereby missing a whole array of situations this diagnosis cause. Many children show other signs of ADHD than fidgeting, talking excessively or running around.

ADHD is a chronic condition marked by persistent inattention, hyperactivity, and sometimes impulsivity. It begins in childhood and often lasts into adulthood. As many as 2 out of 3 children with ADHD continue to have symptoms as adults.

Questions To Consider:
- Are you familiar with the vast array of situations the diagnosis of ADHD can cause?
- Is your child disruptive or anxious?

Tools You Can Apply:
- Recognize the signs
- Refer the child to a specialist
- Remember to self-manage your reaction

As many as 2 out of 3 children with ADHD continue to have symptoms of ADHD as adults. ADHD can mimic parts of other disorders and is sometimes undiagnosed if the child does not display signs of fidgeting, running around and talking excessively.

Children often feel odd and out of place with other children in their age bracket. Sometimes they keep to themselves and try not to be seen in class. Some develop anger issues and become disruptive in class; others are the class clown. Many times, the child has not been diagnosed or given tools to use to combat unusual feelings and other anomalies. A negative reaction can help cripple the child's ability to see himself differently.

Anxiety can accompany ADHD. In many cases, children who do not display hyperactivity outward and those that do, are plagued by constant thoughts and rapid activity in the brain that keeps them from being able to pay attention or concentrate on what's at hand. With some teachers, these students, are pegged as developmentally delayed.

If they lash out, they are troublemakers. Either way, the child doesn't always get what he or she needs. If you feel your child does not have ADHD, ask your doctor to test them to rule it out.

However, pay attention to your child's behavior and be ready to act when you notice irregularities of any kind.

Journal Your Thoughts Here:

Journal Your Thoughts Here:

THE CAPACITY TO DISAPPEAR

Journal Your Thoughts Here:

Journal Your Thoughts Here:

Let's Get Clinical

DEPRESSION IN YOUTH

Chapter Thirteen

Ch 13 - Ways To Spot Depression

Information You Can Use:

Depression is probably the most identified and the most overlooked illness.

Depression is multi-layered and multi-dimensional as it has so many manifestations. Knowing your child's normal patterns may help in identifying an immediate change.

Changes, especially sudden changes, are always related to something. When you notice a change in your child, investigate it immediately.

Questions To Consider:
- Have you noticed changes in your child?
- Do you question and actively listen?

Tools You Can Apply:
- Don't Ignore What You See
- Don't Be Confused By What You See
- Don't Fail To Respond To What You See

Knowing your child's normal patterns may help in identifying an immediate change. Depression can creep up on a child without any warning.

Events that you think may not affect your child, can be something that causes mild, moderate or severe depression, depending on the situation and the closeness your child has to that situation.

It could be the death of a family member, classmate or family friend. It could be a move away from friends, and what is familiar a divorce, family separations and the list go on. Question your child about how they feel when they encounter events that they are opposed too.

With teens, try to include them in some decision making. Seek help immediately when you notice a marked change in your child. Question, then listen with compassion.

Just because a situation does not affect you, doesn't mean it did not affect your child.

Journal Your Thoughts Here:

Journal Your Thoughts Here:

Journal Your Thoughts Here:

Journal Your Thoughts Here:

Let's Get Clinical

KNOWLEDGE IS POWER

Chapter Fourteen

Information You Can Use:

Power is what you believe - How youth and their parents deal with mental, emotional and situational events are vastly different than how physical illnesses are dealt with. If you get a cold, you could buy over the counter medicine or go to the doctor for antibiotics. More severe illnesses may require a short stay in the hospital or a few stay-at-home days.

Mental and emotional problems are never that simple.

Regardless of your religious affiliations, your belief in a higher power above your own perceived power is necessary.

Questions To Consider:

- Do you believe in a higher power?
- Does your child know their worth?

Tools You Can Apply:

- Believe in your power
- Consult your power
- Follow your power

Ch 14 - Ways To Regain Power

Regardless of your religious affiliations, your belief in a higher power above your own perceived power is necessary. If you believe yourself to be inadequate, what you do daily will validate your belief.

Everyone has the power to change his or her thinking into something productive, cherished and beneficial. Darius Foroux wrote that famous statement that says, "if you can believe it, you can achieve it." Here, we are talking about the power of belief.

All those negative things that glide around in your head every day becomes a part of your belief system.

- "I'm not good enough."
- "I'll never have anything."
- "Life is the pits."
- "Nobody loves me."
- "God isn't real."

People live what they believe. Give your child the gift of believing in their ability to accomplish what they want in life.

As their belief in themselves intensify, their power intensifies as well.

Your belief is your power.

Journal Your Thoughts Here:

Journal Your Thoughts Here:

Journal Your Thoughts Here:

Journal Your Thoughts Here:

Journal Your Thoughts Here:

Journal Your Thoughts Here:

THE CAPACITY TO DISAPPEAR

Conclusion

There is no need to get so involved with your lives that you forget you have little ones that need your attention, guidance, love, and protection. You may think that they are too little to recognize who is or isn't around them, but you are fooling yourself into thinking those little brains are not active. They may not be able to tell you that they missed you or noticed that someone else fed them, but you can believe that the smile that greeted you when you walked in, says exactly that. The act of subconsciously disappearing from your child's life may be a new concept for some, but if you can remember your childhood and those moments that you needed your mother and she wasn't there, it becomes a memorable thing.

I have listened to many adults, mothers particularly, talk about how they had a conflictual, distant or strained relationship with their mothers, how she was rarely available for meaningful conversation, didn't attend their activities at school and never seemed interested in their accomplishments, all while telling me about the problems they have with their daughters. It is rare to find a mother who can quickly put the pieces of learned behavior together.

Now is the time to teach and present your daughters with the tools needed to be different. Know that dedicating your life to being present for your children, is not wasted time, but is instead time well spent in the development of a child who will give back to you what you have given to them, love, power and the ability to be present.

There is hope for a better tomorrow!

About the Author

DR. MARY ELLEN DALE is a former business executive turned mental health professional. Dr. Dale was born in Bedford, Ohio (a suburb of Cleveland). After becoming dissatisfied with helping businesses grow and feeling no self-satisfaction, Dr. Dale's attention shifted to social services.

After working for a low-income housing agency, she became disturbed about low-income families and the struggles they faced maintaining housing and the care of their children. She created the Family Development Center within the agency, to address the problems of disadvantage family life.

Dr. Dale is the mother of four educated children and was a therapeutic foster parent for more than twelve years. Dr. Dale's experiences as a divorced mother, raising her own children, in contrast to mentoring other people's children, gave her insight into how families can easily become fragmented. She found herself interested in children who suffered from their underprivileged lifestyle.

Dr. Dale received five degrees in the mental health field, including a Ph.D. in interdisciplinary studies with a concentration in clinical psychology. Her work as the clinical director for a runaway and homeless youth program ignited her need to educate and communicate with mothers on how necessary it is to connect with their daughters.

www.ingramcontent.com/pod-product-compliance
Lightning Source LLC
Chambersburg PA
CBHW081458040426
42446CB00016B/3292